Harvest of Gratitude

Harvest of Gratitude

Matthew Petchinsky

Harvest of Gratitude: A Complete Thanksgiving Guide
By: Matthew Petchinsky

Introduction: Setting the Table of Tradition

Thanksgiving, a time-honored holiday celebrated with great reverence across generations, embodies the very essence of gratitude and communal bonding. It's not just a day marked on calendars or a feast that tantalizes our taste buds; it's a deeply rooted tradition that harkens back to the early settlers and their relationship with the land, community, and spirit of thankfulness. As we prepare to delve into the essence of Thanksgiving, it's important to understand how this celebration has evolved from a historical observance into a cherished cultural fixture.

At its core, Thanksgiving has always been about more than just the meal—it's a day steeped in rituals that create a sense of belonging and continuity. From the moment the first autumn leaves blanket the ground to the final farewell on Thanksgiving night, the holiday is shaped by acts of preparation, connection, and celebration that bind families and friends together. Every dish, every decoration, and every moment shared holds the potential to revive old traditions and inspire new ones, enriching the fabric of our lives.

This guide, "Harvest of Gratitude," is designed to accompany you through the many facets of Thanksgiving. It's a celebration of the harvest season, family ties, and heartfelt traditions. But to truly set the table for Thanksgiving, one must look beyond the turkey and cranberry sauce to the deeper layers of history and meaning that have transformed this holiday into what it is today.

The Historical Roots of Thanksgiving

The origins of Thanksgiving trace back to the early 17th century when European settlers arrived on North American shores seeking new opportunities and freedom. Their survival and eventual prosperity were made possible by the help and guidance of Native American tribes, who taught them to cultivate crops and sustain themselves through harsh winters. The famous feast of 1621, shared between the Pilgrims of Plymouth Colony and the Wampanoag people, laid the foundation for the modern Thanksgiving, celebrating a successful harvest and unity across cultural divides.

Over the centuries, Thanksgiving evolved from sporadic harvest festivals to a nationally recognized holiday. President Abraham Lincoln's 1863 proclamation, made during the heart of the Civil War, established Thanksgiving as an official holiday, calling for a day of thanks and healing across the divided nation. This moment in history transformed Thanksgiving into a day set aside not just for gratitude but for reflection and reconciliation.

Modern Traditions Rooted in the Past

While Thanksgiving has grown in scale and diversity over the years, many aspects of the holiday still echo its historical origins. The focus on seasonal dishes such as turkey, stuffing, squash, and pumpkin pie stems from the crops available during the original celebrations. Sharing a meal remains at the heart of Thanksgiving, symbolizing nourishment not only of the body but of the spirit.

Modern traditions, from the televised Macy's Thanksgiving Day Parade to the ritual of watching football games, reflect the changing nature of the holiday while maintaining its central theme: bringing people together. The holiday is also a time to express thanks for the blessings of the past year, engage in charitable acts, and gather with loved ones to create lasting memories.

Setting the Stage for Your Thanksgiving Celebration

To truly set the table for Thanksgiving, one must start by embracing both the nostalgic and the contemporary aspects of the celebration. This means drawing inspiration from family recipes passed down through generations, incorporating seasonal elements into your décor, and fostering an atmosphere that invites stories, laughter, and togetherness. Whether you're hosting a grand feast for extended family or a cozy meal for a few friends, the intention behind each element can make the celebration special.

Think of this guide as your companion, weaving together practical advice, creative ideas, and thoughtful reflection to make this Thanksgiving one for the ages. From tips on creating the perfect feast to incorporating gratitude rituals that resonate, each chapter aims to enhance your celebration and help you set the table of tradition with purpose and joy.

Let's embark on this journey together, where every chapter deepens your understanding and appreciation of Thanksgiving, helping you craft a celebration that honors tradition while embracing the present. Whether you're a seasoned host or new to hosting your first Thanksgiving, this guide promises to enrich your experience and illuminate the path toward a truly unforgettable holiday.

As you set the table, take a moment to reflect on what Thanksgiving means to you and your loved ones. For at its heart, Thanksgiving is a reminder that no matter where we come from or what challenges we face, there is always something to be grateful for, and there is always room at the table for warmth, generosity, and love.

Chapter 1: The Roots of Thanksgiving: A Journey Through History

Thanksgiving, as it is celebrated today, is a holiday woven from the threads of history, legend, and evolving cultural practices. While many view it as a quintessentially American holiday defined by turkey dinners, parades, and football, its origins paint a rich and complex picture of resilience, gratitude, and collaboration. To truly understand and appreciate Thanksgiving, one must delve into its beginnings and trace the path it has taken over centuries to become a cherished tradition.

The First Thanksgiving: Fact vs. Fiction

The story of the "First Thanksgiving" often conjures images of Pilgrims in buckled hats sitting amicably with Native Americans at a long table piled high with turkey and pies. While this depiction is rooted in truth, it is simplified and, at times, romanticized. The real story is far more nuanced and speaks to themes of survival, alliance, and shared humanity.

In 1620, a group of religious separatists known as the Pilgrims set sail from England aboard the *Mayflower*, seeking freedom to practice their beliefs. They landed at Plymouth Rock, in what is now Massachusetts, after a harrowing 66-day voyage. The Pilgrims arrived late in the season, ill-prepared for the harsh winter that awaited them. Sickness and exposure claimed the lives of nearly half of the settlers by the time spring arrived.

The Pilgrims' survival was due in large part to the assistance of the Wampanoag people, who had inhabited the region for thousands of years. Under the leadership of Chief Massasoit, the Wampanoag forged a strategic alliance with the settlers. One of the most critical figures in this alliance was Tisquantum, commonly known as Squanto, a member of the Patuxet tribe. Having been previously captured, enslaved, and brought to Europe before making his way back to his homeland, Squanto was fluent in English and taught the Pilgrims crucial agricultural techniques such as planting corn and using fish as fertilizer.

The first Thanksgiving feast is believed to have taken place in the fall of 1621, after the Pilgrims' first successful harvest. Historical accounts, such as those of Edward Winslow and William Bradford, suggest that this gathering was a three-day festival that included a variety of foods, games, and celebrations. The Wampanoag brought five deer to the feast, supplementing the Pilgrims' supply of wildfowl, fish, and harvested crops. While turkey might have been part of the spread, it was not the star of the show; venison, ducks, and other game likely took center stage. Additionally, many of the dishes we associate with Thanksgiving today—such as cranberry sauce and pumpkin pie—would not have been present, as the settlers lacked sugar and the means to create such complex dishes.

From Harvest Feast to National Holiday

For many decades following the initial celebration, Thanksgiving was observed sporadically and at the discretion of individual colonies and states. It was not until the late 18th and early 19th centuries that the holiday began to take on a more uniform character. Various states celebrated their own versions of Thanksgiving, often with religious overtones and themes of communal gratitude.

The true champion of Thanksgiving as a national holiday was Sarah Josepha Hale, a prolific writer and editor best known for authoring the nursery rhyme "Mary Had a Little Lamb." For over 17 years, Hale campaigned tirelessly for a national day of thanks, writing to presidents, governors, and influential figures. Her efforts culminated in 1863, when President Abraham Lincoln, amidst the turmoil of the Civil War, issued a proclamation declaring Thanksgiving a national holiday to be observed on the last Thursday of November. Lincoln's proclamation emphasized unity and healing, hoping to soothe the nation's deep wounds by fostering gratitude and reflection.

The Evolution of Thanksgiving Traditions

As the 19th century turned into the 20th, Thanksgiving evolved from a modest religious observance into a grand cultural event. With the Industrial Revolution, families were more dispersed, making holidays like Thanksgiving an important time for gathering. This period saw the emergence of many modern traditions, such as the centerpiece turkey dinner. By the mid-20th century, the concept of "the traditional Thanksgiving meal" had solidified, including turkey, stuffing, mashed potatoes, cranberry sauce, and pumpkin pie as staples.

The holiday also began to be associated with acts of charity and community service. Soup kitchens and charitable organizations used Thanksgiving as an opportunity to provide for the less fortunate, reinforcing its theme of gratitude by encouraging people to give back to their communities.

Thanksgiving parades, most notably the Macy's Thanksgiving Day Parade, became a celebrated tradition in the 1920s. Initially created as a marketing spectacle to draw crowds and launch the Christmas shopping season, the parade has become a cherished spectacle featuring larger-than-life balloons, musical performances, and a festive atmosphere.

Football, too, became an integral part of Thanksgiving in the 20th century. The tradition started with college football games but quickly spread to professional teams. By 1934, the Detroit Lions hosted their first Thanksgiving Day game, and this annual event has been a mainstay ever since, further embedding football into the holiday's fabric.

Thanksgiving in the Modern Era

Today, Thanksgiving is celebrated in a multitude of ways that reflect the diverse tapestry of American society. For many, it remains a day rooted in family, food, and tradition. However, Thanksgiving has also become an occasion for reflection on its historical context. The holiday, while cherished, is a reminder of the complex relationship between early European settlers and Native American tribes. In recent decades, Native American communities have used Thanksgiving as a platform to educate the public about their history and advocate for broader recognition of their culture and contributions.

Incorporating these reflections into Thanksgiving celebrations can enrich the holiday, making it not just a day of feasting but one of deeper understanding and acknowledgment. It is an opportunity to appreciate the resilience, hospitality, and cooperation that made the first Thanksgiving possible, while also recognizing the importance of empathy, inclusion, and dialogue in shaping the holiday as it stands today.

The Enduring Spirit of Thanksgiving

The roots of Thanksgiving are undeniably deep, spreading through centuries of change, conflict, and growth. What began as a modest harvest festival has evolved into a holiday that encompasses family, gratitude, charity, and even national identity. The essence of Thanksgiving is not static; it is an ever-adapting reflection of society's values and collective experiences.

Whether through sharing a bountiful feast, engaging in acts of service, or simply taking time to express gratitude for life's blessings, Thanksgiving invites us to reconnect with what truly matters. It is an occasion to pause, appreciate, and extend our thanks—not just for the food on the table but for the people who share it with us and the traditions that enrich our lives.

In the chapters that follow, we will explore how to bring the spirit of Thanksgiving to life, from the perfect meal to meaningful rituals and thoughtful hosting. With a deeper understanding of the holiday's origins, you can embrace each Thanksgiving with a sense of history, pride, and an open heart that sets the stage for gratitude that extends well beyond a single day.

Chapter 2: Creating the Perfect Thanksgiving Feast: Recipes and Tips

Thanksgiving is synonymous with indulgent, hearty meals that bring loved ones together around a bountiful table. While tradition calls for certain staples, the art of crafting a memorable Thanksgiving feast lies in perfecting recipes that blend classic flavors with contemporary touches. This chapter will guide you through the process of creating a perfect Thanksgiving feast, from planning and preparation to recipes that will wow your guests.

Planning and Preparation: The Foundation of Success

Before diving into recipes, preparation is key. Proper planning will ensure a seamless cooking experience and reduce the stress often associated with hosting.

1. **Menu Planning**: Start by selecting the dishes you'll prepare. Balance is essential: pair rich dishes with lighter sides to create a well-rounded meal. A traditional Thanksgiving menu typically includes:
   - **Main Course**: Roasted turkey or a vegetarian/vegan alternative.
   - **Sides**: Stuffing, mashed potatoes, cranberry sauce, roasted vegetables, and casseroles.
   - **Desserts**: Pumpkin pie, pecan pie, or apple crisp.
2. **Ingredient List**: Compile an ingredient list and check your pantry for existing items to minimize last-minute grocery runs.
3. **Timeline**: Create a cooking schedule that outlines when each dish should be prepped and cooked. Remember, some dishes can be prepared a day or two in advance, such as cranberry sauce or pies.

Recipes for a Show-Stopping Thanksgiving Feast
The Perfect Roast Turkey
Ingredients:

- 1 whole turkey (12-14 pounds)
- 1/2 cup unsalted butter, softened
- 2 tbsp fresh thyme, chopped
- 2 tbsp fresh rosemary, chopped
- 1 tbsp fresh sage, chopped
- 1 lemon, halved
- 1 head of garlic, halved crosswise
- Salt and black pepper to taste
- 4 cups chicken or turkey stock

Instructions:

1. **Prep the Turkey**: Preheat the oven to 325°F (165°C). Remove giblets from the turkey, rinse, and pat dry with paper towels.
2. **Herb Butter**: Mix softened butter with thyme, rosemary, and sage. Carefully loosen the skin over the turkey breast and spread half the butter mixture under the skin. Rub the remaining butter over the skin.
3. **Season and Stuff**: Season the cavity with salt and pepper. Stuff with lemon halves and garlic.
4. **Roast**: Place the turkey on a rack in a roasting pan. Pour 2 cups of stock into the bottom of the pan. Roast for 3 to 3.5 hours, basting every 30 minutes with pan drippings and additional stock as needed. The turkey is done when a thermometer inserted into the thickest part of the thigh reads 165°F (74°C).
5. **Rest**: Allow the turkey to rest for 30 minutes before carving to ensure juicy, tender meat.

Classic Sausage and Herb Stuffing
Ingredients:

- 1 loaf of day-old bread, cut into 1-inch cubes (about 10 cups)
- 1 lb Italian sausage, casing removed
- 1 cup onion, finely chopped
- 1 cup celery, diced
- 2 tbsp fresh parsley, chopped
- 1 tbsp fresh sage, chopped
- 2 tsp fresh thyme leaves
- 1/2 cup unsalted butter
- 2 cups chicken stock
- Salt and black pepper to taste

Instructions:

1. **Preheat the Oven**: Set the oven to 350°F (175°C).
2. **Sauté the Sausage and Vegetables**: In a large skillet over medium heat, cook the sausage until browned, breaking it apart as it cooks. Add onion and celery, cooking until softened (about 5 minutes). Stir in parsley, sage, and thyme.
3. **Combine Ingredients**: In a large mixing bowl, combine the bread cubes, sausage mixture, and melted butter. Gradually add chicken stock until the stuffing is moist but not soggy. Season with salt and pepper.
4. **Bake**: Transfer the stuffing to a greased baking dish and bake for 25-30 minutes or until the top is golden and crispy.

Creamy Garlic Mashed Potatoes
Ingredients:

- 3 lbs Yukon Gold potatoes, peeled and cut into chunks
- 1/2 cup unsalted butter
- 4 cloves garlic, minced
- 1 cup heavy cream, warmed
- Salt and white pepper to taste

Instructions:

1. **Boil Potatoes**: Place potatoes in a large pot and cover with salted water. Bring to a boil and cook for 15-20 minutes or until fork-tender.
2. **Infuse Butter**: While potatoes cook, melt butter in a small saucepan over medium heat. Add garlic and cook until fragrant but not browned.
3. **Mash and Mix**: Drain potatoes and return to the pot. Mash with a potato masher or ricer. Stir in the garlic butter and warm cream. Season with salt and white pepper to taste.

Sweet and Tangy Cranberry Sauce
Ingredients:

- 12 oz fresh cranberries
- 1 cup granulated sugar
- 1/2 cup orange juice
- 1/2 cup water
- Zest of 1 orange

Instructions:

1. **Simmer the Sauce**: In a medium saucepan, combine cranberries, sugar, orange juice, and water. Cook over medium heat, stirring occasionally, until the cranberries begin to pop (about 10 minutes).
2. **Finish with Zest**: Remove from heat and stir in orange zest. Let cool completely before serving to allow flavors to meld.

Tips for the Perfect Thanksgiving Feast

1. **Prep Ahead**: Make dishes like cranberry sauce and desserts a day or two ahead to reduce day-of stress.
2. **Delegate Tasks**: If you're hosting a large gathering, don't hesitate to ask guests to bring a dish or help with setup.
3. **Serve Warm Dishes Together**: Use warming trays or insulated carriers to ensure all hot dishes reach the table at the same temperature.
4. **Carve with Care**: Use a sharp knife and carve the turkey against the grain for maximum tenderness.
5. **Table Presentation**: Elevate your feast with a beautifully set table. Incorporate seasonal elements like gourds, leaves, or candles for an inviting ambiance.

Signature Desserts to End the Feast
Classic Pumpkin Pie
Ingredients:

- 1 unbaked 9-inch pie crust
- 1 can (15 oz) pumpkin puree
- 3/4 cup brown sugar
- 2 tsp cinnamon
- 1/2 tsp ground ginger
- 1/4 tsp ground cloves
- 3 large eggs
- 1 cup evaporated milk
- Whipped cream for serving

Instructions:

1. **Preheat and Prep**: Preheat oven to 350°F (175°C). Place pie crust in a pie dish.
2. **Make the Filling**: In a mixing bowl, whisk together pumpkin, brown sugar, cinnamon, ginger, and cloves. Add eggs one at a time, then gradually stir in evaporated milk until smooth.
3. **Bake**: Pour filling into crust and bake for 45-50 minutes or until the center is set. Let cool before serving.

Making the Feast Unforgettable

A Thanksgiving feast is more than just food; it is an experience steeped in tradition and warmth. Thoughtful planning and preparation can transform your meal from a simple dinner to a cherished memory. Infuse your cooking with care, and don't be afraid to personalize classic dishes with your own unique twist. Whether you're hosting for the first time or continuing a long-held tradition, each dish you serve contributes to the spirit of gratitude and togetherness that defines Thanksgiving.

Chapter 3: Table Settings and Décor Ideas to Elevate Your Holiday

A Thanksgiving feast is as much a visual experience as it is a culinary one. The ambiance set by thoughtful table settings and festive décor can elevate the celebration, making your gathering feel warm, welcoming, and memorable. In this chapter, we'll explore comprehensive ideas and tips to transform your table and dining space into a holiday masterpiece that resonates with the spirit of Thanksgiving.

The Importance of Table Setting and Décor

A beautifully set table creates a sense of occasion and signals to your guests that they are part of something special. The right décor can inspire conversation, enhance the dining experience, and make the holiday feel truly magical. It's more than just plates and cutlery; it's about layering elements that evoke warmth, gratitude, and festivity.

Establishing Your Thanksgiving Theme

Before you begin planning your table settings and decorations, decide on an overarching theme. Some popular themes include:

- **Rustic Harvest**: Natural textures like burlap, woven baskets, and wood accents paired with autumnal colors like burnt orange, deep red, and gold.
- **Elegant Minimalist**: Crisp white tablecloths, delicate centerpieces, and metallic touches for a sophisticated look.
- **Vintage Charm**: Heirloom china, antique candlesticks, and lace runners for a nod to tradition.
- **Nature-Inspired**: Elements like pinecones, acorns, and small branches create an organic feel that brings the outdoors in.

Essential Elements of a Thanksgiving Table Setting

1. Table Linens

Start with a base layer that sets the tone. Tablecloths, runners, and placemats form the foundation of your table décor.

- **Tablecloths**: Opt for fabrics like linen or cotton in neutral tones if you want other elements to stand out, or choose patterned or colored cloths for a more vibrant approach.
- **Table Runner**: A table runner adds a touch of elegance and breaks up the visual monotony of a full tablecloth. Choose one that complements your overall theme.
- **Placemats**: Layering placemats under plates adds texture and helps delineate each guest's space.

Tip: Mix textures for visual interest, such as pairing a rustic burlap runner with sleek, metallic placemats.

2. Dinnerware and Flatware

Choosing the right plates and cutlery can set the stage for a feast that feels special.

- **Plates**: Use your best dinnerware or mix and match for an eclectic look. White or neutral plates allow food to be the main attraction, while colored or patterned plates can add a festive touch.
- **Flatware**: Gold or silver flatware can elevate the setting, giving it a touch of luxury.
- **Charger Plates**: These decorative plates sit under dinner plates and add depth to the table. Metallic chargers, such as gold or copper, are especially fitting for Thanksgiving.

3. Glassware

Having an array of glassware not only looks beautiful but also accommodates different beverages.

- **Water Goblets**: Essential for every place setting.
- **Wine Glasses**: Include red and white wine glasses if you're serving wine.
- **Specialty Glasses**: Consider using glasses for signature cocktails or sparkling cider.

Centerpieces That Steal the Show

The centerpiece is the focal point of your table and can vary in style, height, and complexity. Here are a few centerpiece ideas:

- **Floral Arrangements**: Use seasonal flowers such as sunflowers, chrysanthemums, or marigolds. Incorporate greenery like eucalyptus or rosemary for an aromatic touch.
- **Candle Displays**: Candles provide warmth and a cozy atmosphere. Use a mix of pillar candles, votives, and tapered candles at varying heights for a dynamic look.
- **Harvest Displays**: Arrange pumpkins, gourds, and squashes of various sizes and colors down the center of the table. Add accents like pinecones, acorns, and sprigs of wheat for a harvest-themed display.
- **Edible Centerpieces**: Create a cornucopia filled with fruits, nuts, and vegetables that guests can enjoy during the meal.

Tip: Keep centerpieces low enough so that guests can see and talk to each other across the table.

Personal Touches: Place Cards and Napkin Presentation
1. Place Cards

Place cards add a personal touch and can help avoid confusion about seating. They can be as simple or elaborate as you like:

- **Natural Place Cards**: Use small pumpkins or leaves with guests' names written in calligraphy.
- **Handmade Cards**: Craft cards from cardstock and decorate them with fall-themed stamps or drawings.
- **Mini Easels**: For a more refined touch, use mini easels to display place cards.

Tip: Adding a personal message of gratitude on the back of each place card can make guests feel extra special.

2. Napkin Presentation

Napkins don't just serve a functional purpose; they can also contribute to your décor.

- **Folded Elegance**: Fold napkins into shapes like leaves, fans, or simple pockets to hold silverware.
- **Napkin Rings**: Choose rings that match your theme, such as wooden rings for a rustic look or metallic ones for an elegant feel.
- **Tied with Twine**: Wrap napkins with a piece of twine and tuck a small sprig of rosemary or a cinnamon stick for a fragrant touch.

Enhancing the Atmosphere with Décor Beyond the Table

Decorating your dining room can extend the festive feel throughout your home.

- **Garlands and Wreaths**: Drape garlands of fall leaves or greenery along your dining room hutch or mantel. Hang a fall-themed wreath near the dining area to enhance the theme.
- **Chair Accents**: Tie ribbons, small wreaths, or bundles of wheat to the backs of chairs for added detail.
- **Ambient Lighting**: Incorporate string lights or fairy lights to give the space a soft, warm glow.
- **Seasonal Accents**: Scatter small decorative items like acorns, small pinecones, or decorative leaves on sideboards and window sills.

Creating a Sensory Experience

To make the dining experience even more immersive, consider how you can engage all five senses.

- **Scent**: Use candles or diffusers with fall scents like cinnamon, apple, or pumpkin spice.
- **Sound**: Curate a playlist of soft music or instrumental autumn tunes to play in the background.
- **Taste**: Apart from the meal, offer palate-cleansers like a cranberry or citrus sorbet between courses.
- **Touch**: Use textured table linens and napkins to add a tactile element.
- **Sight**: Ensure there is a balance between well-lit spaces and cozy, dim areas to create the perfect dining ambiance.

Final Touches for a Cohesive Table Setting

As you put the finishing touches on your table, take a step back and look at the overall setup. Ensure that colors are balanced and that each place setting is uniform. Check that there is enough space for serving dishes and that the décor isn't overcrowded.

Remember that the goal is to create an inviting space where your guests can enjoy each other's company and the delicious meal before them. Whether your style is casual and cozy or formal and refined, these table setting and décor tips will help you create an environment that embodies the heart of Thanksgiving: warmth, gratitude, and connection.

Chapter 4: Family Traditions: Activities to Make Memories Last

Thanksgiving is more than just a time for sharing a meal; it is an opportunity to create cherished memories through family traditions and activities. These traditions can be the foundation of family bonds, connecting generations and creating a sense of continuity. In this chapter, we will explore a variety of Thanksgiving activities that foster togetherness, laughter, and gratitude, ensuring that your holiday is not only filled with good food but also with meaningful experiences.

The Importance of Family Traditions

Family traditions are the rituals and practices passed down through generations, shaping the way holidays are celebrated. They create a sense of belonging and stability, provide opportunities for storytelling, and help each family member feel connected to a larger history. Incorporating unique and engaging activities into your Thanksgiving holiday ensures that it is remembered fondly and that new stories are shared for years to come.

Activities to Start and Maintain Thanksgiving Traditions

1. The Gratitude Circle

Overview: A gratitude circle is a simple yet profound activity that encourages every guest to share what they are thankful for. It reminds everyone that Thanksgiving is about gratitude and reflection as much as it is about food.

How to Do It:

- Gather everyone in a circle before or after the meal.
- Pass around a "gratitude token" such as a small pumpkin or decorative item. Each person takes a turn holding the token and shares one thing they are thankful for.
- For a twist, write down the shared thoughts and compile them into a yearly "Thankfulness Journal" that can be read and added to each Thanksgiving.

Tips: If you have young children, encourage them to draw a picture of what they are grateful for and share it with the group.

2. Thanksgiving Scavenger Hunt

Overview: A scavenger hunt adds an element of fun and excitement, especially for families with young children. It encourages exploration and teamwork and is a great way to keep everyone entertained while the food is cooking.

How to Do It:

- Create a list of holiday-themed items to find, such as mini pumpkins, decorative leaves, acorns, or Thanksgiving figurines.
- Hide these items around your home or yard.
- Divide participants into teams or allow them to play individually. The first to find all items on the list wins a small prize.

Tips: Add clues or a map for older children and adults to make the hunt more challenging.

3. Family Recipe Swap

Overview: This tradition helps preserve family culinary heritage by sharing cherished recipes that have been passed down through generations. It's a meaningful way to share family history and ensure that beloved dishes are celebrated long into the future.

How to Do It:

- Ask each family member or guest to bring a printed or handwritten recipe for one of their favorite Thanksgiving dishes.
- Compile these recipes into a family cookbook that can be updated each year.
- Discuss the origins of each dish and share stories about when it was first made or enjoyed.

Tips: If your family is tech-savvy, create a digital version of the recipe collection with photos and family stories to share online or print out.

4. Thanksgiving Talent Show

Overview: A talent show is a lighthearted way to let everyone, especially children, showcase their unique skills and talents. It can include singing, dancing, comedy, magic tricks, or storytelling.

How to Do It:

- Set a designated time for the show, ideally after dinner.
- Provide a "stage" area with a backdrop or decorative frame for photos.
- Encourage participants to perform solo or in groups.
- Hand out awards such as "Best Comedian," "Best Dancer," or "Most Creative Performance" for fun.

Tips: Have a video camera or phone ready to record the performances so they can be watched in future years or shared with family members who couldn't attend.

Creative Thanksgiving Activities for All Ages
5. Thanksgiving Arts and Crafts Table

Overview: Set up a crafts table where guests can create Thanksgiving-themed decorations or keepsakes. This activity is perfect for kids and adults alike and provides a great way for family members to chat and bond while being creative.

Ideas for Crafts:

- **Gratitude Tree**: Provide paper leaves for guests to write what they are thankful for, then attach the leaves to a large branch or wooden stand.
- **Turkey Handprints**: Have younger children make handprint turkeys with paint and paper.
- **Pumpkin Decorating**: Offer paint, markers, and embellishments for guests to decorate mini pumpkins.
- **DIY Place Cards**: Guests can make their own personalized place cards with decorative touches like stamps, dried flowers, or glitter.

Tips: Ensure there are supplies for all age groups, from simple coloring for young kids to more intricate craft kits for adults.

6. Thanksgiving Memory Jar

Overview: A Thanksgiving memory jar is a keepsake that captures the special moments of the day. Over time, it becomes a cherished part of the holiday, filled with memories that can be revisited year after year.

How to Do It:

- Provide slips of paper and pens for guests to write down their favorite moment of the day or a cherished Thanksgiving memory.
- Fold the slips and place them in a decorative jar or container.
- Read a few memories aloud after dinner or save them for the next Thanksgiving to reminisce.

Tips: Encourage guests to date their memories so you can track the evolution of your family traditions over time.

7. Thanksgiving Game Night

Overview: Game night is a perfect way to engage all generations and keep the energy lively. From board games to custom Thanksgiving trivia, there's something for everyone.

Game Ideas:

- **Thanksgiving Bingo**: Create bingo cards with holiday-related items like "turkey," "pumpkin pie," and "family photos."
- **Turkey Trivia**: Prepare a list of fun facts and historical questions related to Thanksgiving.
- **Charades**: Include holiday-themed prompts such as "cooking a turkey" or "watching a parade."

Tips: Choose games that can accommodate different age groups or have simpler rules so everyone can join in.

Building Traditions for a Lifetime

Establishing Thanksgiving traditions that resonate with your family's unique interests and dynamics helps keep the holiday fresh and meaningful year after year. The goal is to create activities that everyone looks forward to participating in, weaving laughter and connection into the fabric of the celebration. These activities not only strengthen family bonds but also create a sense of continuity that spans generations.

Ending the Day with Reflection

As the evening winds down, consider closing your Thanksgiving with a quiet moment of reflection. A candle-lighting ceremony, where each guest lights a candle and shares a hope or wish for the upcoming year, can be a beautiful way to end the festivities. This ritual serves as a gentle reminder of gratitude, hope, and the shared aspirations that bind families and friends together.

Chapter 5: Gratitude Rituals: Cultivating a Season of Thankfulness

Thanksgiving is fundamentally a celebration of gratitude—a time to pause, reflect, and give thanks for the blessings in our lives. While the feast and festivities often take center stage, it's the underlying spirit of thankfulness that makes the holiday truly special. Establishing gratitude rituals can enrich the Thanksgiving experience, fostering deeper connections among family and friends and instilling a sense of mindful appreciation. In this chapter, we'll explore various gratitude rituals that you can incorporate into your Thanksgiving celebration to cultivate a season of thankfulness.

The Power of Gratitude: Why It Matters

Gratitude is more than just a fleeting feeling; it's a practice that has the power to transform our mindset and enhance our well-being. Studies have shown that regularly expressing gratitude can lead to numerous benefits, including improved mental health, stronger relationships, and increased happiness. Thanksgiving provides the perfect opportunity to establish rituals that focus on appreciation and reflection, allowing us to anchor ourselves in the present and connect more deeply with those around us.

Gratitude Rituals to Enrich Your Thanksgiving

1. The Gratitude Jar Tradition

Overview: A gratitude jar is a simple yet powerful way to capture what each person is thankful for. This ritual can be done individually or as a group activity.

How to Implement:

- Set up a large jar or decorative container in a central location, along with slips of paper and pens.
- Throughout the day, encourage guests to write down something they are thankful for and place it in the jar.
- Before or after the Thanksgiving meal, take turns reading some of the gratitude notes aloud.
- At the end of the evening, seal the jar and save it as a keepsake or open it the following Thanksgiving to reflect on last year's blessings.

Tips: For an added touch, use colored paper or cards that match your Thanksgiving theme.

2. The Gratitude Tablecloth

Overview: The gratitude tablecloth is a tradition that doubles as a meaningful decoration. Over the years, it becomes a tapestry of memories and heartfelt messages.

How to Implement:

- Use a plain white or light-colored fabric tablecloth as the base. Fabric markers or pens can be provided for guests to write on the cloth.
- Before or after the meal, invite guests to write a note of thanks or share a meaningful memory.

- Each year, add new messages to the tablecloth, creating a living document of your family's gratitude over time.

Tips: If you'd like to protect the tablecloth, you can place a clear plastic cover over it during the meal.

3. The Morning Gratitude Walk

Overview: A morning gratitude walk is an excellent way to start the day with intention and mindfulness. This ritual helps clear the mind and prepares everyone for the rest of the day.

How to Implement:

- Gather those who wish to participate and take a walk in a nearby park, trail, or even around the neighborhood.
- Encourage participants to share what they are thankful for as they walk or to simply reflect silently on their blessings.
- Conclude the walk by gathering for a moment of collective reflection, where each person shares one thing they noticed or appreciated during the walk.

Tips: This activity is perfect for all ages and provides a calm, meditative start to what can be a busy day.

4. The Gratitude Toast

Overview: A gratitude toast is a heartfelt moment during the Thanksgiving meal where everyone raises a glass in acknowledgment of their blessings.

How to Implement:

- Before the meal begins, the host can kick off the gratitude toast by sharing what they are most thankful for.
- Invite each guest to raise their glass and share a brief word of gratitude.
- The toast can be simple, focusing on one word or phrase, or more elaborate, depending on what feels natural for your group.

Tips: For a playful variation, assign each person a theme for their toast, such as "most surprising blessing" or "funniest moment of the year."

Group Gratitude Practices for Families and Friends

5. Thankful Tree

Overview: A thankful tree is a visual representation of gratitude that guests contribute to throughout the day.

How to Implement:

- Create or purchase a small, branch-like centerpiece to serve as the tree. Alternatively, draw a tree outline on a large piece of paper and hang it on a wall.
- Provide cutout paper leaves in various colors and pens for guests to write down what they are thankful for.
- Attach the leaves to the tree using string or clips, creating a beautiful and meaningful display.
- At the end of the evening, take a moment to read the leaves aloud and appreciate the collective gratitude.

Tips: This can be a recurring activity each Thanksgiving, adding to the display year after year.

6. Gratitude Chain

Overview: A gratitude chain is a fun and interactive way to display thankfulness. It's perfect for families with children but enjoyable for all ages.

How to Implement:

- Cut strips of paper and ask guests to write down something they are thankful for on each strip.
- Loop and staple the strips together to create a chain that can be draped around the room or across the table.
- By the end of the day, the chain will be a colorful reminder of everyone's gratitude.

Tips: Use the chain as decoration throughout the holiday season as a visual representation of your family's thankfulness.

7. Gratitude Letter Exchange

Overview: This activity encourages deeper reflection by having guests write letters expressing their gratitude to another person at the table.

How to Implement:

- Provide stationery, envelopes, and pens.
- Assign each guest a partner or allow them to choose someone they'd like to write to.
- Ask them to write a letter highlighting why they are grateful for that person and specific moments or qualities they appreciate.
- Exchange letters after the meal or at the end of the evening.

Tips: This activity can be emotional and bonding, so be sure to create a comfortable space for guests to express themselves.

Solo Gratitude Practices to Embrace the Spirit of Thanksgiving

For those who prefer quieter or more personal ways to express gratitude, solo rituals can be just as powerful.

8. Gratitude Journaling

Overview: Journaling is a private and introspective way to capture your thoughts of thankfulness. It can be a great morning or evening activity.

How to Implement:

- Set aside a special journal to use each Thanksgiving or throughout the holiday season.
- Spend 10-15 minutes writing down what you are thankful for, moments that brought you joy, and things you look forward to.
- Reflect on your journal entries in the future or use them as inspiration for other gratitude practices.

Tips: Add sketches, photographs, or clippings to make your gratitude journal more personal and visually appealing.

9. Mindful Meditation and Reflection

Overview: A few moments of quiet meditation can center your thoughts and help you appreciate the present.

How to Implement:

- Choose a peaceful space where you won't be disturbed.
- Sit comfortably, close your eyes, and focus on your breath.
- Reflect on what you are grateful for, allowing each thought to fill you with a sense of warmth and contentment.
- Spend 5-10 minutes in this state before opening your eyes and joining the rest of your Thanksgiving activities.

Tips: Incorporate soothing background music or nature sounds to enhance your meditation.

Creating a Legacy of Gratitude

Incorporating these gratitude rituals into your Thanksgiving celebration helps transform it from a simple holiday meal into a meaningful day of connection, reflection, and shared joy. The practices highlighted in this chapter are designed to be adaptable, so you can choose the ones that resonate most with your family and traditions. Over time, these rituals can become the cornerstone of your Thanksgiving celebrations, fostering a sense of gratitude that lingers long after the day has passed.

Chapter 6: Hosting with Ease: How to Manage Guests and Gatherings

Hosting Thanksgiving can be both rewarding and overwhelming. While it's an opportunity to gather friends and family under one roof and create lasting memories, the logistics can be daunting. The key to a successful Thanksgiving is organization, preparation, and the ability to enjoy the day as much as your guests. In this chapter, we'll cover all aspects of hosting with ease, from planning and inviting guests to ensuring everyone feels welcomed and at home.

Preparing for the Big Day: The Host's Checklist

The foundation of any successful gathering is thorough preparation. Here's a step-by-step guide to make sure you're ready for the day.

1. Create a Guest List

Overview: The guest list will help you determine the scale of your preparations. Whether it's an intimate gathering or a large family reunion, knowing who will be attending is essential for planning.

Tips:

- Send invitations early, either by mail, email, or phone, to allow guests ample time to RSVP.
- Confirm any dietary restrictions or preferences to accommodate your guests' needs.
- Have a clear idea of seating arrangements to ensure everyone has a place at the table.

2. Plan the Menu

Overview: A well-thought-out menu is crucial for hosting a memorable Thanksgiving. Balance traditional favorites with new recipes to keep things interesting.

Tips:

- Include dishes that can be made ahead of time to reduce stress on the day of the event.
- Consider adding options for guests with dietary restrictions, such as gluten-free stuffing or vegan sides.
- Plan for a variety of beverages, including non-alcoholic options, cocktails, and hot drinks like apple cider or spiced tea.

3. Organize Your Cooking Schedule

Overview: Timing is everything in the kitchen. A cooking schedule helps ensure that every dish is ready when it's supposed to be.

Tips:

- Break down your cooking into stages: items to prep the night before, dishes that can be cooked in the morning, and those that need to be made right before serving.
- Use timers and alarms to keep track of cooking times and avoid overcooking or burning.
- Enlist the help of family members or friends for simple tasks like chopping vegetables or stirring sauces.

Setting Up the Perfect Space for Your Guests

Creating an inviting and functional space is key to making guests feel comfortable and at home. Here's how to set up your space with ease.

1. Arrange Seating and Tables

Overview: Proper seating arrangements can foster conversation and ensure everyone has a pleasant experience.

Tips:

- Use name cards to help guests find their seats quickly and mix people who don't know each other well to encourage mingling.
- If you're short on seating, consider renting chairs or setting up a kids' table for the little ones.
- Make sure there's ample space between chairs for guests to move comfortably.

2. Set Up a Self-Serve Drink Station

Overview: A self-serve drink station allows guests to help themselves, freeing up your time for other hosting duties.

Tips:

- Include a variety of options such as water, soft drinks, wine, and cocktails. Consider a signature drink that matches the season, such as cranberry punch or mulled wine.
- Label all drinks and provide garnishes, ice, and appropriate glassware.
- Place the station away from high-traffic areas to avoid congestion.

3. Create Cozy Spaces for Conversation

Overview: Not all guests will want to sit at the table the entire time. Create cozy areas where people can relax and chat.

Tips:

- Arrange comfortable seating areas with couches, chairs, and throw pillows.
- Add small side tables for guests to place drinks or plates.
- Set up a few games, puzzles, or conversation starter cards to encourage interaction.

Hosting Strategies for a Smooth Thanksgiving

Managing guests and activities is essential for a seamless event. Here are some strategies to ensure everything goes smoothly.

1. Welcome Guests Warmly

Overview: The way guests are greeted sets the tone for the entire event.

Tips:

- Greet each guest at the door with a warm smile and a brief introduction if they don't know everyone.
- Offer to take coats and direct them to where they can relax and mingle.
- Consider a small welcome drink or appetizer tray at the entrance to make guests feel immediately included.

2. Manage the Flow of Food

Overview: Keeping the food flowing smoothly ensures that guests are satisfied and that the table isn't overcrowded.

Tips:

- Serve dishes buffet-style if you have a large gathering, or pass dishes around the table for smaller groups.
- Have serving utensils ready for each dish and clearly label any items with potential allergens.
- Replenish items as needed and keep track of when certain dishes might need warming up or refreshing.

3. Use a Schedule for Activities

Overview: Plan activities and transitions throughout the evening to maintain energy and engagement.

Tips:

- Schedule a time for the meal, followed by a gratitude ritual, and then games or entertainment.
- Make announcements so guests know when activities are starting, such as a toast or a group game.
- Allow flexibility in the schedule to accommodate conversations and spontaneous moments.

Troubleshooting Common Hosting Challenges

Even the best-laid plans can hit a few bumps. Here's how to handle some common hosting challenges:

1. Dealing with Late Arrivals

Overview: Late arrivals can disrupt the timing of a meal and seating arrangements.

Tips:

- Have appetizers or finger foods ready for latecomers so they can catch up without delaying the main meal.
- Seat guests who have arrived on time and start the meal after a reasonable wait. Politely integrate late arrivals without making them feel uncomfortable.

2. Handling Dietary Restrictions

Overview: Catering to dietary restrictions can feel overwhelming but is essential for making all guests feel included.

Tips:

- Clearly label all dishes, noting if they contain common allergens such as nuts, dairy, or gluten.
- Prepare at least one vegan or vegetarian main dish and sides to ensure inclusivity.
- Notify guests with restrictions in advance about available options and ask if they would like to contribute a dish they can enjoy.

3. Managing Unexpected Guests

Overview: Last-minute additions can happen. Being prepared to accommodate extra guests will save you stress.

Tips:

- Keep extra servings of food on hand, such as rolls, salad, or side dishes that can be quickly prepared.
- Set aside extra place settings that can be easily added to the table.
- Maintain a relaxed attitude and make everyone feel welcome, as Thanksgiving is about inclusivity and sharing.

Ensuring the Host Has a Good Time Too

Hosting doesn't mean you should miss out on enjoying the celebration. Here's how to take care of yourself while managing the gathering.

1. Accept Help

Overview: Don't be afraid to accept offers of help from guests. It can make the day easier and more enjoyable for everyone.

Tips:

- Assign specific tasks like setting the table, serving drinks, or clearing dishes.
- Designate a trusted family member or friend as your co-host to manage smaller details while you focus on larger tasks.
- Remember, most people enjoy contributing and being part of the process.

2. Take Moments to Enjoy

Overview: Throughout the day, carve out moments where you can step back and enjoy the event.

Tips:

- Schedule brief breaks for yourself to enjoy the meal, chat with guests, or relax for a moment.
- Be present during key moments like the gratitude ritual or dessert service to create lasting memories.
- Capture moments with photos or videos, or designate someone to document the event for you.

Post-Meal Hosting: Keeping the Energy Up

Once the meal is over, hosting duties shift to ensuring guests remain engaged and comfortable. Here's how to transition smoothly from dinner to evening activities.

1. Clear the Table Efficiently

Overview: Clearing the table quickly but calmly can help transition to the next phase of the gathering.

Tips:

- Have a few guests help with clearing dishes, but avoid doing all the cleanup immediately—enjoying your time with guests is more important.
- Use disposable containers for leftovers and offer guests the option to take food home.
- Play some light background music to maintain a relaxed atmosphere during the cleanup.

2. Offer Post-Dinner Treats and Drinks

Overview: A coffee and dessert bar is a great way to keep the evening lively and extend the enjoyment of the day.

Tips:

- Set up a station with coffee, tea, hot chocolate, and small desserts like cookies or pie slices.
- Offer after-dinner liqueurs or seasonal drinks like spiced rum or eggnog.
- Include non-sweet options like fruit or nuts for those who prefer lighter fare.

Wrapping Up the Evening

As the event comes to a close, it's important to end on a warm note. Thank your guests for coming and wish them a safe journey home. If you're hosting overnight guests, prepare guest rooms with fresh linens and small comforts like water bottles and snacks. A thoughtful farewell leaves a lasting impression and ensures your Thanksgiving is remembered as a time of genuine hospitality and joy.

Chapter 7: Thanksgiving on a Budget: Frugal yet Festive Ideas

Thanksgiving is a time to celebrate and gather, but the costs associated with hosting a holiday feast can add up quickly. The good news is that with a little creativity and smart planning, you can host a beautiful and memorable Thanksgiving without breaking the bank. This chapter will guide you through various strategies, from budget-friendly menu ideas and decoration hacks to savvy shopping tips and cost-saving entertainment options. Hosting Thanksgiving on a budget doesn't mean sacrificing quality or festivity—it's about making the most of what you have and finding clever ways to stretch your resources.

Smart Menu Planning on a Budget

The biggest expense for any Thanksgiving gathering is often the food. Careful planning can help you serve a feast that is both delicious and affordable.

1. Choose Affordable Staples

Overview: Focus on simple, hearty dishes that use cost-effective ingredients while still maintaining traditional flavors.

Tips:

- **Turkey Alternatives**: If a whole turkey is outside your budget, consider serving a turkey breast or thighs instead. Other affordable protein options include chicken or ham.
- **Hearty Sides**: Sides like mashed potatoes, roasted root vegetables, and green beans are cost-effective and filling.
- **Stretch Dishes**: Casseroles such as green bean casserole or sweet potato casserole can be made in large batches at a low cost and serve many people.

Budget-Friendly Recipe Example: Classic Herb-Roasted Chicken

- Ingredients: Whole chicken, dried herbs, garlic, lemon, butter, and salt.
- Instructions: Season the chicken with herbs, garlic, lemon juice, and butter. Roast in the oven until golden brown and juicy.

2. Incorporate Seasonal Produce

Overview: Using seasonal produce not only adds freshness but also helps keep costs down.

Tips:

- Purchase vegetables and fruits that are abundant during the fall, such as squash, pumpkins, sweet potatoes, and apples.
- Visit local farmers' markets close to closing time for potential discounts on produce.
- Use root vegetables like carrots, parsnips, and potatoes for soups and stews that can be made in large quantities at a low cost.

Budget-Friendly Recipe Example: Roasted Root Vegetable Medley

- Ingredients: Carrots, potatoes, parsnips, olive oil, rosemary, and salt.
- Instructions: Toss chopped vegetables with olive oil, rosemary, and salt. Roast at 400°F (200°C) for 25-30 minutes until tender and golden.

Cost-Saving Shopping Strategies

Grocery shopping for Thanksgiving can be costly if not approached strategically. Here are some ways to shop smarter.

1. Plan Ahead and Make a List

Overview: A detailed shopping list can prevent impulse buys and help you stick to your budget.

Tips:

- Plan your menu and make a comprehensive list of all ingredients needed.
- Check your pantry for items you already have to avoid duplicates.
- Stick to the list while shopping to avoid being tempted by non-essential items.

2. Shop Sales and Use Coupons

Overview: Taking advantage of store promotions and coupons can lead to significant savings.

Tips:

- Look for weekly sales in store flyers and plan your shopping around discounted items.
- Use digital coupons and cashback apps like Ibotta or Fetch Rewards for additional savings.
- Consider shopping at discount grocery stores or wholesale clubs for bulk items.

3. Buy Generic Brands

Overview: Generic or store-brand items often offer the same quality as name-brand products but at a lower price.

Tips:

- Purchase generic staples such as canned goods, flour, sugar, and spices.
- Compare the ingredients on the label to ensure the quality matches your needs.

Decorating on a Dime

Festive decorations can transform your space and set the mood, but they don't have to cost a fortune. Here's how to create a beautiful Thanksgiving atmosphere on a budget.

1. DIY Decorations

Overview: Handmade decorations not only save money but also add a personal touch to your Thanksgiving celebration.

Tips:

- **Natural Elements**: Collect leaves, pinecones, and acorns from outside to create a rustic centerpiece. Spray-paint them gold or bronze for an elegant touch.
- **Mason Jar Centerpieces**: Fill mason jars with candles, cranberries, or small pumpkins for a simple yet chic table display.
- **Paper Crafts**: Use construction paper to create paper turkeys, leaf garlands, or thankful banners.

2. Repurpose and Reuse

Overview: Use items you already have at home and repurpose them into new decorations.

Tips:

- Turn old tablecloths into runners or napkins.
- Use leftover fabric scraps to make small wreaths or bows for chairs.
- Decorate with empty wine bottles by painting them or adding twine and fall foliage.

3. Affordable Centerpieces

Overview: A centerpiece doesn't have to be extravagant to make an impact.

Tips:

- Create a simple centerpiece with a bowl of fresh apples, pears, or small pumpkins.
- Use candles of different heights for an elegant and cozy glow.
- Combine branches and twigs from your yard with fairy lights for a natural and whimsical look.

Entertainment Without Extra Expense

Keeping guests entertained doesn't have to come with a hefty price tag. Simple and fun activities can create a festive atmosphere without added costs.

1. Classic Board Games and Card Games

Overview: Dust off the board games and card decks you already own for some after-dinner fun.

Tips:

- Choose games that are easy to learn and can accommodate multiple players.
- Set up a few game stations so guests can choose which game they'd like to play.

2. Thanksgiving Movie Marathon

Overview: A movie marathon is a relaxed way to wind down the evening, and it's cost-free if you already have access to streaming services.

Tips:

- Pick family-friendly Thanksgiving classics or comedies that everyone will enjoy.
- Set up a cozy viewing area with blankets and pillows.

3. DIY Photo Booth

Overview: A photo booth is a fun addition that guests of all ages can enjoy. Create your own with minimal supplies.

Tips:

- Hang a sheet or a roll of craft paper as a backdrop and decorate it with leaves, pumpkins, or banners.
- Provide props like hats, scarves, and Thanksgiving-themed items for guests to pose with.
- Use a smartphone with a timer function or a camera on a tripod to capture photos.

Hosting Hacks for Maximum Savings

In addition to planning and decorating, there are a few hosting hacks that can help you save money without compromising the quality of your event.

1. Potluck-Style Thanksgiving

Overview: A potluck allows guests to contribute to the meal, reducing your overall expenses and workload.

Tips:

- Coordinate with guests ahead of time to ensure a variety of dishes without duplicates.
- Assign specific courses or types of dishes (e.g., salads, desserts, sides) to each participant.
- Be prepared to provide essentials like the main dish and drinks if you're the host.

2. Simplified Menu

Overview: A more focused menu can reduce costs and the stress of cooking multiple dishes.

Tips:

- Limit the number of side dishes and desserts to a few favorites that everyone loves.
- Consider serving a main dish that's filling and simple, such as a turkey and stuffing casserole.
- Prepare make-ahead dishes to save time and reduce last-minute expenses.

3. Energy Savings

Overview: Hosting can lead to increased utility bills, but there are ways to minimize this.

Tips:

- Cook multiple dishes in the oven at the same time to save on electricity.
- Use a slow cooker or pressure cooker for sides like mashed potatoes or stuffing.
- Rely on natural light during the day and use energy-efficient LED lights in the evening.

Post-Thanksgiving Cost-Saving Tips

Even after the holiday, there are ways to continue saving and reduce waste.

1. Creative Leftover Ideas

Overview: Transform Thanksgiving leftovers into new meals to extend their use and reduce food waste.

Recipe Ideas:

- **Turkey Soup**: Use turkey bones to make broth and add vegetables, noodles, or rice for a hearty soup.
- **Stuffing Muffins**: Mix leftover stuffing with beaten eggs, spoon into a muffin tin, and bake for a quick breakfast or snack.
- **Cranberry Sauce Smoothie**: Blend leftover cranberry sauce with yogurt and frozen fruit for a refreshing post-holiday treat.

2. Freeze Extras

Overview: Preserve extra food by freezing it for future meals.

Tips:

- Portion out turkey, casseroles, and soups into freezer-safe containers.
- Label and date each container for easy reference.
- Use leftovers within three months for the best flavor and quality.

Conclusion: Celebrating with Joy, Not Stress

Thanksgiving on a budget doesn't mean sacrificing quality, comfort, or joy. With thoughtful planning, creative solutions, and a focus on the true spirit of the holiday—gratitude and togetherness—you can host a beautiful and meaningful celebration. By implementing these cost-saving tips, you'll not only create a memorable day for your guests but also enjoy the satisfaction of knowing you hosted a warm and festive Thanksgiving without straining your finances.

In the next chapter, we'll delve into how to plan for Thanksgiving when you have special dietary needs to consider, ensuring everyone feels included and satisfied at the table.

Chapter 8: Special Diets and Thanksgiving: Inclusivity at the Table

Thanksgiving is a holiday that embodies the spirit of unity and celebration. However, as the diversity of dietary preferences and restrictions increases, hosting a feast that caters to everyone can feel daunting. Whether your guests are vegetarian, vegan, gluten-free, or have other dietary needs, it's essential to ensure that each person at the table feels seen, respected, and included. In this chapter, we will delve into creating a Thanksgiving spread that embraces inclusivity while maintaining the festive flavors and atmosphere that everyone loves.

Understanding the Importance of Inclusive Dining

Inclusivity at the dinner table goes beyond simply having options—it's about making sure that every guest feels welcome and cared for. This starts with understanding why dietary preferences and restrictions exist:

- **Health Reasons**: Some guests may need to avoid specific foods due to allergies, intolerances, or health conditions like celiac disease or diabetes.
- **Ethical Choices**: Vegetarians and vegans choose to exclude animal products for ethical, environmental, or personal beliefs.
- **Religious Practices**: Some dietary restrictions are influenced by religious beliefs that must be respected.
- **Lifestyle Preferences**: Individuals might choose diets like keto or paleo to support their health and wellness goals.

Tips for Planning an Inclusive Thanksgiving Menu
1. Gather Dietary Information Early
Overview: Before planning your menu, communicate with your guests to find out about any dietary restrictions or preferences they may have.
Tips:

- Send out a group message or include a note in your invitation requesting guests to inform you of their dietary needs.
- If possible, ask for examples of dishes they enjoy that fit their dietary requirements to inspire your planning.
- Consider asking a few guests with specific dietary needs to contribute a dish they love.

2. Plan a Flexible Menu
Overview: Build a menu that is adaptable and includes dishes that can be easily modified to meet different dietary needs.
Tips:

- Prepare dishes that are naturally inclusive, such as salads with dressings on the side or roasted vegetables seasoned simply.
- Use plant-based alternatives for common ingredients, such as swapping butter with plant-based margarine or chicken stock with vegetable broth.
- Have a variety of side dishes that can serve as mains for guests with dietary restrictions.

Detailed Recipes for Special Diets

Below, we've included a selection of recipes that cater to common dietary needs while maintaining the spirit of Thanksgiving.

1. Vegan Stuffed Squash

Dietary Accommodation: Vegan, gluten-free (with gluten-free breadcrumbs)

Ingredients:

- 2 acorn squashes, halved and seeded
- 1 cup cooked quinoa
- 1/2 cup chickpeas, rinsed and drained
- 1/4 cup dried cranberries
- 1/4 cup chopped walnuts
- 2 tbsp olive oil
- 1 tsp ground cinnamon
- Salt and black pepper to taste

Instructions:

1. Preheat oven to 400°F (200°C). Brush squash halves with olive oil, sprinkle with salt, and place cut-side down on a baking sheet. Roast for 25 minutes or until tender.
2. In a bowl, mix cooked quinoa, chickpeas, cranberries, walnuts, cinnamon, salt, and pepper.
3. Fill the roasted squash halves with the quinoa mixture and return to the oven for 10 minutes. Serve warm.

Tips: Substitute the quinoa with rice or wild rice for a different texture and flavor.

2. Gluten-Free Cornbread
Dietary Accommodation: Gluten-free, vegetarian
Ingredients:

- 1 cup gluten-free cornmeal
- 1 cup gluten-free flour blend
- 1/4 cup granulated sugar
- 1 tbsp baking powder
- 1/2 tsp salt
- 1 cup milk (or plant-based milk for dairy-free)
- 1/3 cup vegetable oil
- 2 large eggs (or flaxseed eggs for vegan)

Instructions:

1. Preheat oven to 375°F (190°C) and grease a baking dish.
2. In a mixing bowl, combine the cornmeal, flour, sugar, baking powder, and salt.
3. In another bowl, mix the milk, oil, and eggs. Add the wet ingredients to the dry ingredients and stir until just combined.
4. Pour the batter into the prepared dish and bake for 20-25 minutes or until a toothpick comes out clean. Let cool before serving.

Tips: Add chopped jalapeños or shredded dairy-free cheese for a flavor twist.

3. Dairy-Free Mashed Potatoes

Dietary Accommodation: Dairy-free, vegan
Ingredients:

- 3 lbs Yukon Gold potatoes, peeled and cut into chunks
- 1/2 cup unsweetened almond milk (or any plant-based milk)
- 1/4 cup olive oil or dairy-free butter
- 2 cloves garlic, minced (optional)
- Salt and black pepper to taste

Instructions:

1. Boil potatoes in a pot of salted water for 15-20 minutes, or until fork-tender.
2. Drain the potatoes and return them to the pot.
3. Add the almond milk, olive oil, and garlic. Mash until smooth.
4. Season with salt and pepper. Serve warm.

Tips: For a creamier texture, use a hand mixer to blend the potatoes.
Modifying Traditional Dishes to Meet Dietary Needs
1. Stuffing:

- **Vegan Option**: Use vegetable broth and swap butter for olive oil. Include vegetables, herbs, and dried fruit for flavor.
- **Gluten-Free Option**: Use gluten-free bread or cornbread to maintain the texture.

2. Gravy:

- **Vegan Option**: Make a rich mushroom gravy by sautéing mushrooms, adding vegetable broth, and thickening with cornstarch.
- **Gluten-Free Option**: Use cornstarch or arrowroot powder instead of flour to thicken the gravy.

3. Pumpkin Pie:

- **Dairy-Free Option**: Replace evaporated milk with coconut milk or almond milk.
- **Gluten-Free Option**: Use a gluten-free pie crust or make a crustless version.

Buffet-Style Serving for Inclusivity

Serving dishes buffet-style is an effective way to manage various dietary needs without complicating the dining experience.

Benefits:

- Guests can choose dishes that fit their preferences.
- Labels can be placed in front of each dish to indicate if it's vegan, gluten-free, nut-free, etc.
- A buffet reduces the need for complicated table service and allows guests to customize their plates.

Tips for a Successful Buffet:

- Organize dishes in sections (e.g., gluten-free section, vegan section) for easy navigation.
- Keep sauces and dressings on the side so guests can control their intake.
- Provide separate serving utensils for each dish to avoid cross-contamination.

Creating a Welcoming Environment for All

Overview: Setting the stage for an inclusive Thanksgiving goes beyond food—it's about creating an atmosphere where all guests feel comfortable and respected.

Tips:

- **Inform Guests About Options**: Let your guests know which dishes cater to specific dietary needs.
- **Avoid Spotlighting Dietary Restrictions**: Serve all dishes with equal importance to avoid making guests with restrictions feel singled out.
- **Be Open to Questions**: Be knowledgeable about the ingredients in your dishes and be ready to answer questions.

Handling Cross-Contamination Concerns

For guests with severe allergies or celiac disease, preventing cross-contamination is essential.

Precautions:

- Use separate cutting boards, utensils, and cookware for dishes that cater to specific dietary needs.
- Clearly label dishes that are free of common allergens.
- Prepare allergy-friendly dishes first and keep them covered until served.

Budget-Friendly Ideas for Dietary Alternatives

Dietary accommodations can sometimes come with added costs, but there are ways to manage these expenses:

Tips:

- **Buy in Bulk**: Purchase items like gluten-free flour and dairy-free milk in bulk to save money.
- **Make It from Scratch**: Homemade dishes are often more cost-effective than specialty store-bought items.
- **Simplify**: Focus on one or two main dishes that meet dietary needs and round out the menu with simple sides.

Conclusion: A Table for Everyone

Creating an inclusive Thanksgiving doesn't have to be overwhelming or costly. By planning ahead, being mindful of your guests' needs, and incorporating simple but thoughtful changes, you can host a Thanksgiving that is welcoming to all. The effort you put into accommodating everyone at your table will not only be appreciated but will also foster an environment of warmth, togetherness, and genuine hospitality.

Chapter 9: Beyond Thanksgiving: Planning for a Smooth Holiday Transition

Thanksgiving marks the start of a busy holiday season filled with celebrations, gatherings, and preparations. The transition from Thanksgiving to the rest of the holiday season can often feel overwhelming, with a rapid shift from one festivity to another. To make this transition smooth and enjoyable, thoughtful planning and organization are essential. This chapter will guide you through post-Thanksgiving strategies, effective home organization, holiday preparation, and ways to keep the spirit of gratitude alive as you move into the holiday season.

1. Reflecting on Thanksgiving: Preserving the Memories

Overview: Before diving into the next round of holiday preparations, take time to reflect on Thanksgiving and capture the memories created during the day.

Tips:

- **Create a Thanksgiving Memory Book**: Collect photos, gratitude notes, and memorable stories from the day. Add these to a scrapbook or digital photo album.
- **Share Memories**: Encourage guests who attended to share their favorite moments in a group chat or through email. This can be a fun way to relive the holiday.
- **Thank You Notes**: Send thank-you notes to guests or helpers who contributed to making Thanksgiving special. This small gesture extends gratitude and strengthens bonds.

Activity Idea: Host a "Thanksgiving Recap Night" with close family members where you watch videos or go through photos from the day while enjoying leftover pie or hot drinks.

2. Post-Thanksgiving Home Organization

Overview: A clean, organized space is key to transitioning smoothly into the next phase of the holiday season. Tidying up after Thanksgiving can help you reset your home and mind for the upcoming festivities.

Tips:

- **Clean and Store Holiday Decor**: Carefully pack away Thanksgiving decorations and label storage containers for easy retrieval next year.
- **Tackle the Kitchen**: Deep clean the kitchen, focusing on the oven, fridge, and counters. This ensures you have a fresh space for future holiday baking and meal prep.
- **Declutter Common Areas**: Clear out any clutter from living rooms and guest spaces to make room for holiday decorations.
- **Sort Leftovers**: Organize and store leftovers in clear, labeled containers. Freeze what you won't eat within a few days to minimize waste.

Quick Checklist:

- Wash and store table linens, serving dishes, and special dinnerware.
- Check for items that need repairing or replacing before the next holiday.
- Reorganize your pantry to make space for holiday staples like baking supplies and snacks.

3. Extending the Spirit of Gratitude

Overview: Keeping the spirit of Thanksgiving alive can set the tone for a season filled with joy and appreciation.

Tips:

- **Gratitude Calendar**: Create a gratitude calendar that continues through December. Each day, write down one thing you're thankful for as a family. This simple practice can build excitement for the upcoming holidays while keeping gratitude at the forefront.
- **Volunteer as a Family**: Engage in community service, such as serving meals at a local shelter or organizing a food drive. Volunteering fosters a sense of community and extends the Thanksgiving spirit into the holiday season.
- **Kindness Challenges**: Initiate a family "Acts of Kindness" challenge where each member commits to a certain number of kind acts before the end of the year. Share your experiences during family dinners or over hot cocoa.

Activity Idea: Start a "Thankfulness Jar" that stays out until New Year's Eve. Each time someone in the household experiences or witnesses something positive, they write it down and place it in the jar. Read these notes together at the end of the year.

4. Prepping for Holiday Shopping and Gifting

Overview: The transition from Thanksgiving to the December holidays often includes a flurry of gift buying and decorating. Planning your holiday shopping and gifting early can reduce stress and save money.

Tips:

- **Create a Gift Budget**: Set a realistic budget for holiday gifts to avoid overspending. Allocate funds for each person or category (e.g., family, friends, colleagues).
- **Plan Your Shopping List**: Write down gift ideas for each recipient and keep an eye out for post-Thanksgiving sales and discounts. Consider making homemade gifts to add a personal touch.
- **Shop Early and Online**: Take advantage of Black Friday and Cyber Monday sales for discounts on gifts, decorations, and essentials. Shopping online can save time and allow for easier comparison shopping.
- **Gift-Wrapping Station**: Set up a designated space for wrapping gifts, complete with paper, bows, tape, and scissors. This prevents last-minute chaos and keeps supplies organized.

Sustainable Gifting Tip: Use recycled or eco-friendly wrapping paper, fabric wraps, or reusable gift bags for an environmentally conscious holiday season.

5. Transforming Your Space for the Holiday Season

Overview: Transitioning your home from Thanksgiving to the winter holidays can be seamless with some planning and creativity.

Tips:

- **Switch Out Decor Gradually**: Replace fall-themed decor with winter elements such as evergreen garlands, twinkle lights, and cozy textiles. Layering these items creates a natural transition from one season to the next.
- **Keep Some Thanksgiving Decor**: Integrate neutral items, like candles and wooden accents, into your winter setup for continuity.
- **DIY Decorations**: Create holiday decorations as a family using simple, affordable materials. Ideas include homemade wreaths, paper snowflakes, and mason jar centerpieces filled with pinecones and fairy lights.

Activity Idea: Host a "Decorating Day" where family members help decorate the house while listening to holiday music and enjoying seasonal treats like hot chocolate and cookies.

6. Preparing Your Holiday Menu

Overview: Holiday meals are often more elaborate than Thanksgiving, so planning in advance can help you stay organized and stress-free.

Tips:

- **Make a Master Menu**: Plan out your holiday meals, including appetizers, main courses, sides, and desserts. Consider any special dietary needs and incorporate some of your Thanksgiving favorites with a seasonal twist.
- **Batch Cooking**: Prepare dishes that can be made ahead of time and frozen, such as casseroles, sauces, and cookie dough. This will save time during the busiest days of the season.
- **Utilize Leftovers Creatively**: Use Thanksgiving leftovers to create new dishes like turkey pot pie, cranberry sauce parfaits, or sweet potato pancakes.

Budget Tip: Buy non-perishable ingredients in bulk when they are on sale, such as canned goods and baking supplies, to save money on your holiday cooking.

7. Planning Gatherings Beyond Thanksgiving

Overview: The holiday season often includes multiple gatherings with friends, family, and colleagues. Planning these in advance can help reduce the stress of hosting multiple events.

Tips:

- **Simplify Menus for Casual Gatherings**: Keep meals simple with options like a potluck or finger foods for smaller gatherings. This reduces the burden on the host and allows guests to contribute.
- **Plan Themed Nights**: Create themed events like "Ugly Sweater Night," "Hot Cocoa and Movie Marathon," or "Holiday Game Night" for a fun and low-cost way to celebrate.
- **Schedule Rest Days**: Block out a few days between events for rest and recovery to avoid burnout.

Hosting Hack: Prepare a "Guest Kit" with essentials like disposable cutlery, napkins, and serving dishes that you can pull out quickly for last-minute gatherings.

8. Maintaining Your Well-Being During the Holiday Rush

Overview: The transition from Thanksgiving to the holidays can be overwhelming, so it's important to prioritize your well-being.

Tips:

- **Set Realistic Expectations**: Accept that not everything will be perfect and that it's okay to say no to additional commitments if you're feeling stretched thin.
- **Stay Organized**: Use a planner or digital calendar to keep track of upcoming events, grocery lists, gift lists, and to-do tasks.
- **Practice Self-Care**: Dedicate time to unwind with activities that help you recharge, such as reading, meditating, or going for a walk.
- **Delegate Tasks**: Share the workload by involving family members in planning, decorating, or cooking.

Mindfulness Exercise: Take five minutes each morning to list three things you're grateful for and set a simple intention for the day. This can help maintain a positive mindset and keep stress at bay.

9. Sustaining the Holiday Spirit Post-Thanksgiving

Overview: Keeping the holiday spirit alive is about fostering joy, gratitude, and connection throughout the season and beyond.

Tips:

- **Keep Traditions Alive**: Carry forward traditions from Thanksgiving, such as the gratitude jar or family stories, into other holiday gatherings.
- **Create New Traditions**: Introduce new traditions, such as a holiday puzzle that you work on as a family throughout December or a weekly baking night.
- **Stay Connected**: Reach out to friends and family members you may not see during the holidays. Send holiday cards, host virtual meet-ups, or schedule a time to call.

Activity Idea: Host a "New Year's Reflection Night" where family members share their favorite moments from Thanksgiving and the holidays and discuss hopes and goals for the upcoming year.

Conclusion: From Thanksgiving to a Season of Joy

The transition from Thanksgiving to the broader holiday season doesn't have to be stressful or rushed. By taking time to reflect, organize, and plan ahead, you can move smoothly into the rest of the holidays while maintaining the warmth and gratitude that Thanksgiving embodies. With thoughtful preparation, your home will be ready, your spirit will be lifted, and your loved ones will feel cherished throughout the season.

<u>Message from the Author:</u>

I hope you enjoyed this book, I love astrology and knew there was not a book such as this out on the shelf. I love metaphysical items as well. Please check out my other books:

-Life of Government Benefits

-My life of Hell

-My life with Hydrocephalus

-Red Sky

-World Domination:Woman's rule

-World Domination:Woman's Rule 2: The War

-Life and Banishment of Apophis: book 1

-The Kidney Friendly Diet

-The Ultimate Hemp Cookbook

-Creating a Dispensary(legally)

-Cleanliness throughout life: the importance of showering from childhood to adulthood.

-Strong Roots: The Risks of Overcoddling children

-Hemp Horoscopes: Cosmic Insights and Earthly Healing

- Celestial Hemp Navigating the Zodiac: Through the Green Cosmos

-Astrological Hemp: Aligning The Stars with Earth's Ancient Herb

-The Astrological Guide to Hemp: Stars, Signs, and Sacred Leaves

-Green Growth: Innovative Marketing Strategies for your Hemp Products and Dispensary

-Cosmic Cannabis

-Astrological Munchies

-Henry The Hemp

-Zodiacal Roots: The Astrological Soul Of Hemp

- Green Constellations: Intersection of Hemp and Zodiac

-Hemp in The Houses: An astrological Adventure Through The Cannabis Galaxy

-Galactic Ganja Guide

Heavenly Hemp

Zodiac Leaves

Doctor Who Astrology

Cannastrology

Stellar Satvias and Cosmic Indicas

<u>Celestial Cannabis: A Zodiac Journey</u>

AstroHerbology: The Sky and The Soil: Volume 1

AstroHerbology:Celestial Cannabis:Volume 2

Cosmic Cannabis Cultivation

The Starry Guide to Herbal Harmony: Volume 1

The Starry Guide to Herbal Harmony: Cannabis Universe: Volume 2

Yugioh Astrology: Astrological Guide to Deck, Duels and more

Nightmare Mansion: Echoes of The Abyss

Nightmare Mansion 2: Legacy of Shadows

Nightmare Mansion 3: Shadows of the Forgotten

Nightmare Mansion 4: Echoes of the Damned

The Life and Banishment of Apophis: Book 2

Nightmare Mansion: Halls of Despair

<u>Healing with Herb: Cannabis and Hydrocephalus</u>

<u>Planetary Pot: Aligning with Astrological Herbs: Volume 1</u>

Fast Track to Freedom: 30 Days to Financial Independence Using AI, Assets, and Agile Hustles

<u>Cosmic Hemp Pathways</u>

How to Become Financially Free in 30 Days: 10,000 Paths to Prosperity

Zodiacal Herbage: Astrological Insights: Volume 1

Nightmare Mansion: Whispers in the Walls
The Daleks Invade Atlantis
Henry the hemp and Hydrocephalus

10X The Kidney Friendly Diet
Cannabis Universe: Adult coloring book
Hemp Astrology: The Healing Power of the Stars
Zodiacal Herbage: Astrological Insights: Cannabis Universe: Volume 2
<u>Planetary Pot: Aligning with Astrological Herbs: Cannabis Universes: Volume 2</u>
Doctor Who Meets the Replicators and SG-1: The Ultimate Battle for Survival
Nightmare Mansion: Curse of the Blood Moon
<u>The Celestial Stoner: A Guide to the Zodiac</u>
Cosmic Pleasures: Sex Toy Astrology for Every Sign
Hydrocephalus Astrology: Navigating the Stars and Healing Waters
Lapis and the Mischievous Chocolate Bar

Celestial Positions: Sexual Astrology for Every Sign
Apophis's Shadow Work Journal: : A Journey of Self-Discovery and Healing
Kinky Cosmos: Sexual Kink Astrology for Every Sign
Digital Cosmos: The Astrological Digimon Compendium
Stellar Seeds: The Cosmic Guide to Growing with Astrology
Apophis's Daily Gratitude Journal

Cat Astrology: Feline Mysteries of the Cosmos
The Cosmic Kama Sutra: An Astrological Guide to Sexual Positions
Unleash Your Potential: A Guided Journal Powered by AI Insights
Whispers of the Enchanted Grove

Cosmic Pleasures: An Astrological Guide to Sexual Kinks

369, 12 Manifestation Journal

Whisper of the nocturne journal(blank journal for writing or drawing)

The Boogey Book

Locked In Reflection: A Chastity Journey Through Locktober

Generating Wealth Quickly:

How to Generate $100,000 in 24 Hours

Star Magic: Harness the Power of the Universe

The Flatulence Chronicles: A Fart Journal for Self-Discovery

The Doctor and The Death Moth

Seize the Day: A Personal Seizure Tracking Journal

The Ultimate Boogeyman Safari: A Journey into the Boogie World and Beyond

Whispers of Samhain: 1,000 Spells of Love, Luck, and Lunar Magic: Samhain Spell Book

Apophis's guides:

Witch's Spellbook Crafting Guide for Halloween

<u>Frost & Flame: The Enchanted Yule Grimoire of 1000 Winter Spells</u>

<u>The Ultimate Boogey Goo Guide & Spooky Activities for Halloween Fun</u>

Harmony of the Scales: A Libra's Spellcraft for Balance and Beauty

The Enchanted Advent: 36 Days of Christmas Wonders

Nightmare Mansion: The Labyrinth of Screams

Harvest of Enchantment: 1,000 Spells of Gratitude, Love, and Fortune for Thanksgiving

The Boogey Chronicles: A Journal of Nightly Encounters and Shadowy Secrets

The 12 Days of Financial Freedom: A Step-by-Step Christmas Countdown to Transform Your Finances

If you want solar for your home go here: https://www.harborso-lar.live/apophisenterprises/

Get Some Tarot cards: https://www.makeplayingcards.com/sell/apophis-occult-shop

Get   some   shirts: https://www.bonfire.com/store/apophis-shirt-emporium/

<u>**Instagrams:**</u>
@apophis_enterprises,
@apophisbookemporium,
@apophisscardshop
Twitter: @apophisenterpr1
 Tiktok:@apophisenterprise
Youtube: @sg1fan23477, @FiresideRetreatKingdom
Hive: @sg1fan23477
CheeLee: @SG1fan23477

Podcast: Apophis Chat Zone: https://open.spotify.com/show/
5zXbrCLEV2xzCp8ybrfHsk?si=fb4d4fdbdce44dec

Newsletter: https://apophiss-newsletter-27c897.beehiiv.com/

www.ingramcontent.com/pod-product-compliance
Lightning Source LLC
Chambersburg PA
CBHW072110150726
47999CB00005B/1987